A Mind of Her Own

The Story of Mystery Writer
Agatha Christie

Written by

Robyn McGrath

Illustrated by

Liz Wong

BEACH LANE BOOKS

New York   London   Toronto   Sydney   New Delhi

Where has he gone now?
Agatha prowls for clues.

She inspects fallen beechnuts,
spies fresh paw prints,
and listens for a playful bark.

The garden is the perfect setting for one of her stories.
Stories that young Agatha makes up,
  with imaginary friends,
    a family of kittens,
      and her loyal terrier, Tony.

      For Agatha, make-believe is serious work.

"Agatha, always in her head."

Agatha has a mind of her own.

At story time, she hangs
on every word
as Mother spins a yarn,

Nursie tells
a bedtime tale,

or her sister, Madge,
reads her the classics.

But when Agatha tries to write her own ideas on paper . . . the letters and words come out jumbled.

She much prefers arithmetic with her father, turning equations into puzzles for solving.

Agatha's brother and sister are much older,
so Agatha finds ways to entertain herself.

She hides with Tony under the dining table,
quietly noticing everything around the house.

Curious whispers.
  Rosy red cheeks.
    And a mouth turned up . . .
      or down.

What could these clues mean?

Agatha devours gloomy books and delights in detective stories. Ah, these are the perfect puzzles for solving!

Like Sherlock Holmes, Agatha takes on the keen eye of a detective. Secret nooks and shadows hide stories waiting to be uncovered.

Who is knocking at the door?
What are the contents of the letter?
Why does that lady carry a cane?

"Agatha, always in her head."

Agatha has a mind of her own!

When Agatha loses her father,
she wanders the house in a cloud of sorrow.

Eventually, Agatha's mother
sends her to boarding school.

There she learns piano and loves to sing and act.

She dreams of performing

but suffers stage fright.

Setting acting aside, Agatha returns to writing. Time and time again, she puts pen to paper, conducting a symphony of ideas,

but teachers reject her compositions and criticize her grammar.

So Agatha turns to so-called serious work.
She enrolls in first aid classes as a way to help with the war.

As a nurse, she watches the steady hands of doctors,
   follows the solemn faces of wounded soldiers,
      and helps patients craft letters to loved ones.

Back at home, Agatha retreats into her imagination.
The hospital becomes the perfect detailed setting,
and the war heroes her mysterious characters.

Who does that soldier call to in his sleep?

What does the visitor carry in the
covered basket?

Her mind fills with story possibilities . . .

but again the words twist and snag
when she puts pen to paper.

Agatha's older sister, Madge, has always been
known as the clever writer.
She and Agatha debate the mysteries
that fill their bookshelves.

Did you notice that clue?
Was the justice fair?

"I should like to try my hand at a detective story," says Agatha.

"They are very difficult to do," replies Madge. "I bet you couldn't."

But, with a mind of her own . . .

Agatha accepts the challenge.

Putting together one clue at a time, she begins
filling her six-pence notebooks with
suspicious characters,
    fast-paced plots,
        engaging scenes,
            and sharp dialogue.

Agatha's detective story becomes a puzzle for her to solve.
A mathematical equation.
Just like she did with her father!

And the most important puzzle pieces are . . .

Who?

What?

Where?

When?

Why?

How?

JEWELER

NEWS
THIRD
GIRL
DISAPPEARS

INTERNATIONAL
SMUGGLERS
ARRESTED

PALE
HORSE

Agatha finds ideas in store windows,
in newspaper headlines,
and on the London streets.

She overhears a whispered conversation at a tea shop,

catches a curious phrase from a woman on the tram,

spots a squabble between two passing strangers—

all these details bring her characters to life.

She has the foundation of her detective story!
But she's missing one major piece of the puzzle: How?

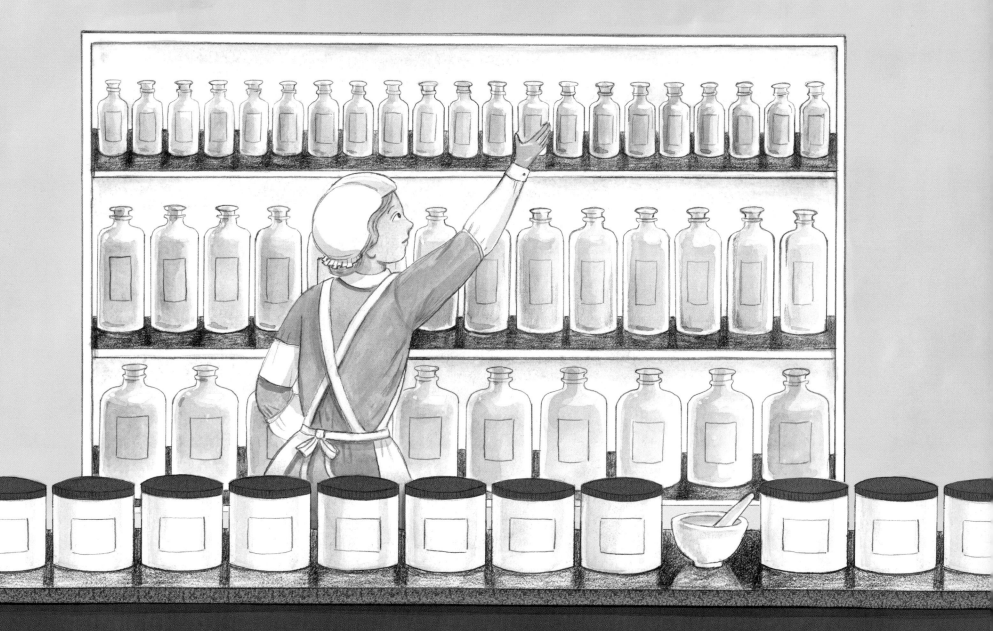

Back at the hospital, this time in the dispensary where medicines are stored,
Agatha surveys the bottles on the shelves.

A wrong dose could easily become deadly. Idle thoughts blend into different combinations. . . .

That's it!
The perfect crime . . .

POISON!

Borrowing Madge's typewriter,
she begins to batter out her story.

Agatha wants to feel her characters
before putting them on the page.
Wandering through the sunlit gardens,
she waves her hands,
speaks in a deep voice,
or feigns surprise.

Her characters come alive
as she acts out their dialogue.

Agatha, always in her head,
carefully pieces together her story.

When should they
notice the lock is broken?
Did the gardener or the
housekeeper commit the crime?
And where will they find the telltale stain?

Agatha explores different patterns and possibilities.
Crafting plot twists and
sprinkling in clues.
How about a double bluff
to keep readers guessing?

Passages cut.
Scenes polished.
The puzzle pieces start
to fall into place.

Then, after years of working out the story in her head,
and reading it over and over,
she is ready.

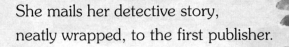

She mails her detective story,
neatly wrapped, to the first publisher.

All too soon,
the manuscript is returned . . .

REJECTED!

With determination, Agatha bundles it off to another publisher.
Again . . .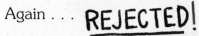

Agatha wonders: Is it truly awful?
   Are her characters not believable?
     The clues confusing?
      Did she misspell a word? Or two?

Not ready to lose hope, she sends it out once more.
   But again it comes back— REJECTED!

Agatha submits the manuscript
one last time!

A year later, an envelope
arrives for Agatha.

Her story is . . .

Finally, Agatha holds her first book.

She continues to fill notebook after notebook
with detailed observations and probable plots.

Nursemaids with hidden identities,
houses on isolated islands,
and crimes on boats and trains
become the perfect mysteries for solving.

Agatha's observing and imagining
and puzzling and plotting
leave readers everywhere searching
for clues to crack her cases!

BOOKSHOP

THEATRE

AGATHA CHRISTIE'S
The Mousetrap

TICKETS

YES, Agatha has a mind of her own!

More about
Agatha Christie

Agatha Miller was born in Torquay, England, on September 15, 1890, to a middle-class family. She was often the only child at home since her brother and sister, Monty and Madge, were more than a decade older. While stories were a large part of Agatha's daily life, her mother believed Agatha shouldn't learn to read until she was eight because she thought it would be better for Agatha not to strain her eyes or over-exert her brain. But Agatha kept the books that were read out loud to her and memorized the words. She secretly taught herself to read by five years old!

With no playmates or formal schooling, Agatha was often alone with her imagination. She spent a great deal of her time with her imaginary friends and family pets, as well as her nursemaid, whom she called Nursie. As a young girl, Agatha was paralyzingly shy. Family often teased Agatha for appearing to be lost in her thoughts.

When Agatha was eleven, her father died. Soon after, Agatha's mother determined that Agatha should attend boarding school. During her succession of schooling in both Torquay and Paris, teachers often criticized Agatha's writing for being too fanciful. She was easily side-tracked and didn't keep to the point, and she found grammar particu-larly difficult. She delighted in acting, singing, and playing the piano,

but her nerves overwhelmed her when performing live. One winter, while Agatha was laid up in bed recovering from influenza, her mother suggested she write stories like her sister, Madge, did. While Agatha still struggled with grammar, she quickly set to writing and put her dreams of being onstage aside. Throughout her teen years, Agatha con-tinued to write poems and short stories, and even had a few poems published in the *Poetry Review*. She finished school in 1910 when she was twenty years old.

In 1912, Agatha met Archie Christie, an aviator, and they were engaged within the year. While Archie was away on the World War I front in France, Agatha took nursing classes and worked with the Voluntary Aid Detachment in a Red Cross hospital in Torquay. It was then that she began writing her first detective story. Agatha married Archie on Christmas Eve, 1914, when she was twenty-four years old. The very next day, Archie returned to the war in France and Agatha returned to her work, this time in the hospital dispensary, where she learned a great deal about medicine.

It took four years for Agatha to work out the plot of her first novel. After submitting her manuscript to publishers, multiple rejections followed. But, a year after sending in her final submission, her manuscript was accepted. That same year, Agatha gave birth to a baby girl, Rosalind. Agatha's first book, *The Mysterious Affair at Styles*, was published in 1920. The story features a beautiful country estate, an injured war hero, lots of suspicious characters, and of course . . . poison!

In 1926, after the decline of her marriage and the death of her mother, Agatha mysteriously disappeared. A nationwide search to find Agatha ensued. Eleven days later, she was found at a spa hotel using a pseudonym—a fake name. The why and how of Agatha's disappear-ance largely remains a mystery.

Agatha got a new start when she traveled by railway on the Orient Express to Baghdad in 1928. On this trip, she met archaeologist Max Mallowan, who became her second husband. Agatha traveled with Max to archaeological digs in the Middle East. Visiting these new places renewed her inspiration and she wrote more than ever.

Though traveling gave Agatha many new ideas for her mysteries, sometimes her prejudices showed in her writing. While audiences can

admire Agatha's stories for their ingenuity and scope, it's also important to be aware of those prejudices when reading her books.

Agatha Christie is often considered the Queen of Crime. Her novels have sold billions of copies, making her the bestselling novelist of all time. She wrote more than sixty detective novels as well as short fiction and plays, and her books have been translated into more than one hundred languages.

Agatha was a writer with an observant eye who penned gripping and entertaining stories. She was not only a famous author but a real adventurist who sought justice in her books. She is known for her character development and great sense of dialogue. Her two most famous characters, detective Hercule Poirot and Miss Marple, have won the hearts of countless readers.

In 1974, she made her last public appearance for the opening night of the film version of her novel *Murder on the Orient Express*. Agatha Christie died on January 12, 1976.

Author's Note

As an only child, I too spent a lot of time with my imagination. I filled many spiral notebooks full of possible story ideas. And like Agatha, I too had trouble with spelling and grammar.

When I decided to research more about this famous mystery writer, Agatha left plenty of clues for me to piece together her life.

—R. M.

Illustrator's Note

While working on this book, I listened to many of Agatha Christie's audiobooks and was inspired to include references to her life and her novels in my illustrations. Agatha Christie fans might recognize references to her book titles, clues, or characters throughout this book in the paintings on the walls, designs on vases, and objects in the rooms. I hope you enjoy spotting these details as much as I enjoyed painting them.

—L. W.

Mystery Vocabulary

alibi: an explanation that a suspect uses to show that they did not commit the crime

clues: hints that can help the reader and the detective solve the mystery. These could include fingerprints, items left at the scene of the crime, or things people say or do.

crime: an act that is against the law

detective, or sleuth: a person who investigates crimes by gathering evidence to solve mysteries

double bluff: an attempt to deceive someone by telling that person the truth when he or she thinks you are telling a lie

evidence: information that is used to prove that a suspect is guilty

red herring: false clues that make the story unclear and throw the detective off track

suspect: a person who is believed to have *possibly* committed the crime

victim: someone who is harmed or suffers because of the crime

witness: someone who saw the crime being committed

For Rob, who always believes in my stories
—R. M.

For Mom and my sister, Jen
—L. W.

Bibliography

Christie, Agatha. *An Autobiography*. New York: William Morrow, 1977.

Cottingham, Matt, dir. *Inside the Mind of Agatha Christie*. PBS, 2021. 45 min.

Curran, John. *Agatha Christie: Murder in the Making: More Stories and Secrets from Her Notebooks*. New York: HarperCollins, 2011.

Curran, John. *Agatha Christie's Secret Notebooks: Fifty Years of Mysteries in the Making*. New York: HarperCollins, 2009.

Davison, Sean, dir. *Agatha Christie: 100 Years of Poirot and Miss Marple*. Honey Bee, 2020. 67 min.

Lewins, Clare, dir. *The Mystery of Agatha Christie with David Suchet*. PBS, 2014. 56 min.

Thompson, Laura. *Agatha Christie: A Mysterious Life*. New York: Pegasus Books, 2018.

For more information about Agatha Christie's life and work, visit agathachristie.com.

BEACH LANE BOOKS • An imprint of Simon & Schuster Children's Publishing Division • 1230 Avenue of the Americas, New York, New York 10020 • Text © 2024 by Robyn McGrath • Illustration © 2024 by Liz Wong • Book design by Karyn Lee © 2024 by Simon & Schuster, LLC • All rights reserved, including the right of reproduction in whole or in part in any form. • BEACH LANE BOOKS and colophon are trademarks of Simon & Schuster, LLC. • Simon & Schuster: Celebrating 100 Years of Publishing in 2024 • For information about special discounts for bulk purchases, please contact Simon & Schuster Special Sales at 1-866-506-1949 or business@simonandschuster.com. • The Simon & Schuster Speakers Bureau can bring authors to your live event. For more information or to book an event, contact the Simon & Schuster Speakers Bureau at 1-866-248-3049 or visit our website at www.simonspeakers.com. • The text for this book was set in ITC Souvenir Std. • The illustrations for this book were rendered in watercolor and then finished digitally. • Manufactured in China • 0124 SCP • First Edition • 10 9 8 7 6 5 4 3 2 1 • Library of Congress Cataloging-in-Publication Data • Names: McGrath, Robyn, author. | Wong, Liz, illustrator. • Title: A mind of her own : the story of mystery writer Agatha Christie / written by Robyn McGrath ; illustrated by Liz Wong. • Description: New York : Beach Lane Books, 2024. | Includes bibliographical references. | Audience: Ages 4-8 | Audience: Grades 2-3 | Summary: "Uncover the fascinating, inspiring, and sometimes-mysterious true story of world-renowned detective novelist Agatha Christie's journey to authorship in this picture book biography"— Provided by publisher. • Identifiers: LCCN 2023032045 (print) | LCCN 2023032046 (ebook) | ISBN 9781665917933 (hardcover) | ISBN 9781665917940 (ebook) • Subjects: LCSH: Christie, Agatha, 1890-1976—Juvenile literature. | Women novelists, English—20th century—Biography—Juvenile literature. | Authors, English—20th century—Biography—Juvenile literature. | LCGFT: Biographies. | Picture books. • Classification: LCC PR6005.H66 Z748 2024 (print) | LCC PR6005.H66 (ebook) | DDC 823/.912 [B]—dc23 /eng/20230718 • LC record available at https://lccn.loc.gov/2023032045 • LC ebook record available at https://lccn.loc.gov/2023032046